Make Money

A Beginners Guide to Start an Online Business, Work from Home, Make Money, and Develop Financial Freedom

By: Anthony J. Fleischmann Jr.

Copyright 2017
American Christian Defense Alliance, Inc.
Baltimore, Maryland
ACDAInc.Org

Dedication

This book is dedicated to all the entrepreneurs out there that refused to accept the status quo and strive ever higher to greater heights. Your dedication, determination, and endurance to persevere through all obstacles is to be admired and emulated.

This book is for you

Forward

This book is written for the complete beginner to the mysterious world of making money online. I have attempted to address the majority of the fundamentals to consider prior to beginning your journey to making money online or working from home.

If you're completely new to making money online this book should jumpstart your journey to success. This book will help you learn to use your computer to make money online and point you in the direction to establishing your financial freedom.

This book also lays out the strategies to consider when working from home and developing your plan for financial freedom. If you need a more flexible schedule, more money in your pocket and have the commitment and dedication - with hard work you can truly succeed

Table of Contents

Dedication..2

Forward...3

Chapter 1: Failure 6

Chapter 2: Start a Legal Business?8

Chapter 3: Your Taxes....................11

Chapter 4: Realistic Expectations
and Goals..14

Chapter 5: Educating Yourself....16

Chapter 6: Your Business Plan....20

Chapter 7: The Right Mentality..23

Chapter 8: Dealing with Family..26

Chapter 9: Investing........................29

Chapter 10: Your Work Space.....33

Chapter 11: Accounts You Need.39

Chapter 12: Your Schedule...........45

Chapter 13: Fighting Against
Distractions..48

Chapter 14: It Works......................52

Chapter 15: Income........................55

Chapter 16: Online Businesses...58

Chapter 17: Picking a Business...69

Chapter 18: Stop Procrastinating and Take Action 73

Special Gift 75

Stay In Contact 77

Find All Our Books 78

Additional Platforms 80

Chapter 1: Failure

Failure is Part of Success!!

Some might wonder why failure is even mentioned in a book about success and making money online. The reality is that failure often times precedes any success that we may have.

Let's look at this objectively – how many of us have succeeded the first time we tried anything? I think if we're honest with ourselves we can acknowledge that we often times fail at something we first try.

However, that failure that we first experience normally doesn't stop us from trying again and ultimately succeeding at whatever we put our mind to.

Numerous entrepreneurs and successful people around the world attest to the fact that they have failed more times than they have succeeded. Look at the autobiographies of those famous individuals within the business world or in any area of life for that matter. What you will normally find are individuals that have fought through the struggles and the hurdles of life to ultimately succeed.

They pressed on regardless of the situation, regardless of the circumstance because they had a vision and a purpose that they were striving to complete. This is more than just goalsetting, this is establishing your vision and your purpose in life and how that will be reflected in the online business that you choose to create. Don't ever let someone tell you that failure is not part of success because it most certainly is.

Chapter 2: Start a Legal Business?

Some of you may be wondering if you need to start a legal business. You may be wondering . . . Do I need to be incorporated, have an LLC, or establish some kind of nonprofit organization. The simple answer is no for the majority of the online businesses that are available to choose from.

Now keep in mind I am in no way a lawyer, nor am I giving any legal advice here. The advice that I give is based on my personal experience and the information that I have gathered as of this writing. If you have serious questions regarding the legality of whether you need to start a legal business, sometimes referred to as a legal entity, you should consult a qualified lawyer regarding the matter. With that being said, let's move on.

Any online business that you start will require some form of identification number, whether that be your Social Security number or your employer identification number which is commonly referred to as your EIN.

My personal experience and calling within the Christian ministry has led me to develop a nonprofit organization that is classified as a nonstock corporation. With the majority of the things that I do online I do use my EIN and have things under the umbrella of the Christian ministry.

However, this is not the case for everything that I do online and is certainly not necessary when you first get started. It does offer an extra layer of protection for you from a legal standpoint, but again it is completely unnecessary when you're first starting out.

Just understand that you will need to fill out tax forms if you will be receiving money from a specific company online or utilizing a company's website to sell products or services. This should be expected and is commonplace - so don't freak out or be nervous about putting your Social Security number on some tax forms, just make sure the company has a solid reputation.

Remember: You don't need to start a legal business but you always, and I mean always treated like a real business – because it is.

Chapter 3: Your Taxes

Understanding Your Taxes

Ah taxes, the one thing no one wants to discuss in any business. The mere thought of taxes often times raises people's blood pressure to questionable heights and a sense of doom. While no one likes to discuss taxes, or even think about taxes for that matter it is important to discuss if you are going to be working from home and making money online with your own business.

As you make money online with your business it's important to save up at least 30% of your net profits for your taxes. Unlike traditional 9 to 5 jobs in which you and your employer pay taxes every time you get paid being self-employed this is just not an option.

Paying taxes at the end of the year may seem like a terrifying thought to you if you have been conditioned by the 9 to 5 grind. Yet I assure you there is nothing to fear. Most entrepreneurs and self-employed people in the United States do this exact same thing each year.

Those that are wise plan things out in a prudent way. They keep all their receipts for business expenses, including such things as their mileage. Having these receipts well organized and in a safe spot will save you a ton of time when working with your accountant. And while we're on the subject of taxes, yes you will need a professional accountant if you want to ensure the maximum benefits available.

A great tip to earn even more
money is to have the 30% of your
net profits in some type of
interest-bearing account to enable
you to earn money throughout the
year prior to utilizing it to pay for
your taxes. So it seems that waiting
until the end of the year to pay
your taxes does have its benefits.

Remember to seek out a qualified
professional accountant prior to
developing your overall plan of
action to gain concrete
information on how to maximize
your money to the fullest.

Chapter 4: Realistic Expectations and Goals

Establishing realistic expectations and goals is a double-edged sword. On one hand you want to have very high expectations and goals for yourself and for your business while at the same time you need to be as realistic as possible to plan accordingly.

One thing I try to do is to set very high goals and expectations for myself and my online business but when I plan, I plan for the worst case scenario. What I mean by that is I always base my planning on the minimum amount of money that I'm expected to make each month.

Another way to look at it is to have very high long-term goals and expectations and very attainable expectations in the short term.

When you're first starting your online business or working from home on a more consistent basis you will face challenges that she didn't even know existed. But I have confidence in you that you are the type of individual that will overcome any challenge or obstacle in your way to achieve your goals.

Chapter 5: Educating Yourself

Learning what you need to know is all part of the journey to successfully starting and maintaining a successful work from home online business. Unfortunately this is the longest part of the entire process yet is no different than anything else that you learned in your life – everything that you've learned has taken a measure of time.

Thankfully there online resources such as this book, audiobooks, and even online courses that you can utilize to learn specific skills related to your online business.

Just watch out for sleazy online "Gurus" that promote their courses. So keep your BS meter on high alert, as there are hustlers and scammers throughout the Internet world trying to take advantage of people just starting out in specific online businesses.

Remember, Jesus said that "we will know them by their fruits".

Going back to realistic expectations ..... Having realistic expectations also transcends to the area of educating yourself on the specifics that you need to know when starting your new online business.

Let's look at the principle of having realistic expectations and goals and how it applies to our normal work life. For those of you that have worked traditional jobs, you understand that there is always a process to learning and developing new skills specifically related to a new job.

In fact companies recognize this as well, this is why you have a probationary period. Normally probationary periods run between three months and six months giving you ample time to learn and master the basic skills specifically related to the job.

If you look at a new employee and compare them to someone who has been on the job for 5, 10 or even 20 years you will immediately notice a huge difference in their skill level. The same holds true for your online business and working from home - the more time that you spend educating yourself and doing the actual work which pertains to your business the more that things will flow and become second nature.

When you reach this level of expertise you'll look at things that were once very difficult in a whole new light.

Educating yourself is an important first step in this entire process – you can't do something new if you don't learn something new. Even if you plan to utilize existing skills there is always going to be a learning curve – how long is completely up to you.

I recommend that you immerse yourself in learning as much as you possibly can in the online business that you choose to start and then after gathering the appropriate knowledge and establishing your plan – take massive action. For without action you're just daydreaming and your goals will never be accomplished.

However, since you're reading this book, since you have taken the first step to educating yourself I know that you're on the right path and I'm confident that your journey will lead you to success.

Keep going – You can do it!

Chapter 6: Your Business Plan

Develop Your Plan and Walk with Wisdom

How will you present yourself to the world, and how will the things that you're doing be interrelated? What are your strategies for marketing and promoting your online business? These are some of the questions that you should be answering in your business plan.

This business plan should be the driving force that steers you to your ultimate and goals. You may need to adjust along the way, and that's perfectly fine, but this needs to be established well in advance.

Not having a business plan is like a blind man walking in heavy traffic – there is bound to be an accident and someone getting hurt. Don't make the mistake of not thinking about your overall plans as they are a key element to achieving your goals.

Part of this plan should include a centralized website in which you point people to. Having a centralized website in which people can come and visit to learn more about your products or services is huge – I daresay it is a must have.

Having a website is great but it's only one part of the puzzle. You need to have your products and services interrelated and marketing each other. This may take a bit of creative planning on your part but it can be done.

It's important to also have a whole systems approach that includes multi layered products and services that overlap one another.

Wherever possible your contact information such as your website address, email, or phone number should be easy to find and if possible within products that you may develop such as a book.

To some degree you also want to have your business plan somewhat secret. You don't want your competition knowing all the ins and outs of how you're doing business. Keep your strategies, tactics, and ninja like techniques of your online business close to your chest.

And since we're talking about ninjas here, I highly recommend the book, the Art of War by Sun Tzu. For many Japanese businessmen it is required reading. The Art of War has strategies that are just as good in the business world as they are in the battlefield – it's all on how you apply the principles found in the book.

Chapter 7: The Right Mentality

What is the right mentality to have when developing an online business that you work from home?

The only way that you would ever know that is if you've done it before and experienced the ups and downs of starting an online work from home business. Thankfully I've been there and done it and put that information here in this book.

Throughout all the highs and the lows that you will experience starting an online business and working form home one of the number one things to have is the right mentality.

We've touched on this briefly when we discussed mental fortitude but this mental fortitude needs to be combined with professionalism. You need to develop within your mind an understanding that what you're doing is a real legitimate business – and you need to treat it like such

When you have the mentality that what you're doing is a real legitimate business it will help you to treat it as such and put in the necessary work required to make the kind of money that you're looking to make.

If your online business is a side hustle, something you do part time you may not be overly concerned with having this mentality but one of the worst things that you could do if you're looking for your online work from home business to be your full time revenue maker is to treat your business like a hobby.

Big goals and big expectations paired with the drive, motivation, and determination that is within you will lead you to great success. Just stay on your grind and don't quit.

Remember your actions will always follow your beliefs so if you're serious about your online business put in the work necessary to be successful and treated like a real job – or better yet a real business.

Chapter 8: Dealing with Family

Family Na-Sayers and Negative People - Mental Fortitude

Dealing with family naysayers and negative people requires a certain level of mental fortitude and resiliency. It is not easy to deal with family members that are doubting you, your vision, and your plan. Anyone who's ever tried to start an online business that has a family knows these challenges all too well.

There are so many reasons that family members and other people in your life may harbor negative feelings towards you or your aspirations. The reality is you may never know the reasons behind their feelings, they may say one thing but in all actuality believe something completely different.

So the idea is not to focus on those individuals in your life that are naysayers and presenting negative energy towards you. The idea is to focus on controlling you and your actions. The simple reality is, no matter how much we may want to be able to control someone's behavior they are ultimately going to do what they want to do. This is why focusing on developing self-discipline and mental fortitude is so critical for your success.

You have to learn how to tune out all those people in your life that tell you, "you can't do it, you shouldn't do it, or why bother". If you have a dream, a vision, or a goal - go out and seize it. Utilize each day to its fullest and work ever closer to those things in which you aspire.

How nice is it going to feel when you can say to all those family members and those negative people in your life who said that'll never work or you should just go out and get a "real job" – a big fat See I told you so!

Being able to be vindicated in the eyes of those naysayers and negative people in your life will boost your confidence like never before and encourage you to take on even greater challenges in the future - but it all starts with a small measure of faith and a big scoop of courage.

The more success you have as you progress with your online businesses the more confidence you will develop along the way. Yet it's that first step that is the most challenging, but oh how sweet is that first success.

Chapter 9: Investing

Investing in You and Your Business

Investing in you and in your future is something that should not cause you any hesitation or fear. When I was going through college I had to take out college loans to help supplement my income. Yet I never looked at this is a bad thing. My thought was always this, "If I don't invest in myself who else will?" See it's a matter of trusting yourself and your abilities and understanding what your potential is.

Don't let a small investment in your business stop you from living up to your potential. If you don't trust yourself now, if you don't have the confidence to take that step of faith through courage you're not ready to start an online business.

What business do you know that starts without investing in the equipment or supplies that it needs to run and operate smoothly – it just doesn't exist

Every business has expenses whether small or great - but they are still expenses. Many online businesses require very little money to get started, if any.

However, it's critical to have the appropriate hardware such as computers, printers, microphones, cameras or whatever other items that you may need. In addition to the hardware, you will want to make sure that you also have the appropriate software within your computer to do whatever is necessary within your business.

Some examples of software that may be needed would be video editing software, audio editing software, or even speech to text software like I'm using now to, "Write this book". Don't underestimate the importance of quality software, it can be a major timesaver and make working from home a lot more pleasant.

In today's high-tech society the price of technology has come down tremendously and is reasonably priced to allow the average entrepreneur access to buying it.

When I first began my journey into entrepreneurship and working from home I did what I had to do to raise the money needed to purchase the equipment that I wanted. In fact I sold my SUV over at CarMax and reinvest the money back into my business. I went without a car for a month or so but the benefits of this bold action continue to benefit me to this very day.

So think about what you might have in your home that you're willing to part with – could you sell it and reinvest that money back into your business?

Understand not all online businesses will need the same equipment or software. But there's a saying where I come from, "Go big or go Home" and that's just how I roll. I typically buy the best that I can afford after doing a good amount of research on what specific product or brand is the best. This is just my personality and is completely not necessary to start an online business or work from home. Buy what you can afford and as you continue to make money take a portion of that money and reinvest it in better equipment and better software.

Just remember when you're investing in yourself, your trusting and believing in yourself and in your own abilities for success.

Chapter 10: Your Work Space

Finding Your Work Space in Your Home

Finding your workspace in your home can be a very challenging experience. I have went back and forth three or four different places within my home trying to find the best possible workspace to conduct my online businesses. I suspect that you may have to go through a bit of trial and error just like I did defined just that right spot in your home.

My Experience Moving Rooms

My experience started in a spare bedroom on the second floor of her home. This was a nice square room with a good amount of light coming through the window.

However, the floor had a few spots that were creaky. I gotta tell you creaking this was driving me nuts.

So I moved downstairs into our living room area and that did not last too long. Way too many distractions not to mention my wife given me the blues about my stuff in the living room.

So to make peace with the wife I traveled down stairs into our basement. Our basement has carpet and drywall but still was a basement and had that basement smell. I endured as long as I could in the basement, even finishing up an online course called, "Martial Arts Ministry for Christian Men".

The major issues the basement, other than the smell was the lack of sunlight and those pesky crickets that seem to want to chirp at the exact time I would try to record anything. So I came to the realization that either me or the crickets needed to go – as you can imagine I journeyed once again to a new location.

However, I kept the downstairs basement area set up for filming online courses, YouTube videos, or whatever else I needed. To be honest there was no other place for me to film in the house so that decision was made due to lack of options more than anything else.

There was just no way for me to fit my three point lighting system, various different backgrounds, my camera, tripod and all the other accessories into any other space in my house in which I could've filmed reasonably well. I guess I'm just gonna have to deal with those crickets after all.

But this time around when I go downstairs I'll be focused specifically on filming and nothing else - which was one of the issues when I was down there as well. You and I and everyone else that has online businesses really need to guard against distractions and getting sidetracked with other things – even if their business related, stay focused.

You may be wondering where I ended up setting up my office again. Well I went back up to the room with the creaky floor. Overall it was the best option, especially sense I have turned the walk-in closet into a recording booth to do voiceovers – so if you need some voiceover work done hit me up with the contact information at the end of this book. I figured that sunlight, fresh air, and the lack of crickets is a good trade-off.

So when you're looking to find a place to put your home office or recording studio try to pick a quiet space with lots of natural light, with fresh air, and that is free from distractions.

There are times you just may need a change in scenery something new and fresh to inspire. If you're getting bogged down consider moving your online work space in your home. Do what you have to do to stay motivated and inspired because all of this must come from within you.

I actually have another laptop set up at the kitchen counter and sometimes I will use that computer just to change up the scenery a little bit. Sometimes I just like the open feel of working at the kitchen countertop as opposed to the office located in the spare bedroom. You may have your own preferences so do what works best for you and your situation with your business.

Wherever you put your office make sure you have things where you can physically see them on a regular basis. I'm a visual person so I will have things on my wall so I can see them on a regular basis either to inspire me, motivate me or just simply let me know that there is a deadline coming up.

Remember less is more when it comes to this specific principle. Don't have your walls looking like a piñata exploded all over them, keep things clean and neat so you can remain organized.

And while we're talking about being well organized, it's important to have a calendar and a whiteboard in your office to keep you on track with the things that you need to do.

On a side note having an accountability buddy is a great way to increase productivity – just thought I'd throw that in there for you.

Chapter 11: Accounts You Need

Your Social Media Accounts and Website

What accounts will you need to start your online business? When you're first starting out you want to make sure that you have all the major social media platforms covered such as:

- Facebook
- Twitter
- LinkedIn
- YouTube

You shouldn't concern yourself too much with other platforms at this time. I know there are several other social media platforms that are gaining in popularity and use but in all reality are completely unnecessary when you first get started.

Your accounts should be set up in such a way that reflects your professionalism, your work ethic, and your products, services, and skills

You want to utilize these social media platforms as a way to connect with those that may wish to buy your products or services.

However, never be a salesman on your social media platforms. Be a real person that gives the people on your platform that connect with you real value in some kind of way without asking for anything in return. In doing this you will develop trust, credibility, and a loyal following. After you have developed these things within the hearts and minds of those on your social media accounts it will be easier to reach out to them when you develop future products or services that they might be interested in – this is what's called warming them up.

I have a sincere dislike for salesman in general. I don't like anyone trying to push a sale on me - so don't be that person. Be the person that helps educate those that link up with you through social media. The more that you educate someone the more likely they are to purchase something from you in the future because they understand the value that you would be giving them.

Additionally your social media platforms should direct all those that link up with you to your website -this is the beginning phases of what is known as branding.

Your website is one of the biggest factors in your overall success when it comes to having an online presence.

What does your website say about you, is it professional or does it make you look like a clown? Having a professional website is your first impression to the world, on to future clients, and on future buyers. A professional website will actually draw more professional individuals to you and make you more money both now and in the future.

Understand your website doesn't need to have a huge amount of pages or content but it does need to be clean, well-organized, and properly laid out. When building a website less is actually more at times. You want your website to give them just enough information about you, or your products or services that they reach out to you in some kind of way.

One of the main things that you need to have on your website is a service that allows you to collect emails from people that visit your site. Collecting these emails will end up being the backbone of your online business and is the start of what is known as email marketing. The company I use is called Aweber and is approximately $20 a month. There are free services out there as well like Mail Chimp but I prefer Aweber due to the simplicity of its interface.

If you do need help developing your website I do have experience in that and would be happy to work with you for reasonable rate. If you mention that you got this information from this book I'll even give you 10% off.

Now for those that do not know, a professional website can actually cost you a few thousand dollars – in fact I've seen prices on average between four to eight thousand dollars. I was actually on a website development committee at the last place I held a traditional job and these were the numbers from the company's that gave proposals.

Don't worry though a simple professional website doesn't need to cost that much. If all you want or need is a simple professional website chances are I can do it for around $500.00 – just hit me up so we can discuss the matter further. Again my contact information is at the end of this book.

Chapter 12: Your Schedule

Setting Up and Sticking to Your Schedule

How many of you who've had traditional jobs were able to set your own schedule or come in whenever you wanted? I would assume that most of you reading this book probably would not be able to come in to work whenever you wanted or set your own schedule.

However this is exactly what you can do when you work from home. The flexibility that you have in creating your own schedule is one added benefit to working from home yet if you don't have "normal business hours" that you work consistently you're not treating this is like a real business.

No successful person can wake up whenever they want, go to sleep whenever they want, or go to work whenever they want. They understand that success is built on establishing good work habits such as creating and sticking to it work schedule.

There are a lot of considerations to think about when establishing your schedule some of these may include:
- Children
- Pets
- Spouses
- Noisy Neighbors
- Family Obligations

Each person will have different considerations to think about as no two people are the same. But make no mistake about it, having a dedicated time to work on your business each day is critical to the success of your online business.

Some of you may be wondering what type of schedule you should create, should you work the normal 9 to 5?

The answer to this is very simple, be available when your customers or clients need you. If you're in the United States and doing business with someone in Japan then your schedule is going to look much different than if you were doing business with someone who also lives in the United States.

Set your schedule up in such a way that you are doing business online during the majority of the time that most of your customers are also doing business online. This is one great way to meet your clients or customers need as fast as possible.

Of course you have flexibility with all of this but always remember the golden rule, "Family Comes First" – especially when prioritizing time.

Chapter 13: Fighting Against Distractions

Staying Focused

I have had my fair share of distractions both physically and in the digital world. As a stay-at-home dad who homeschools, runs multiple online businesses, and has responsibilities for very hyper dog I know all too well how difficult it can be the fight against distractions and stay focused – but it can be done.

It takes a certain level of self-discipline, flexibility, and drive to accomplish your goals and without one of the three components I just mentioned it's going to be virtually impossible to stay focused.

Yet you can actually utilize some of these distractions in a positive way if you "flip the script" so to speak. Let's take for instance my very hyperactive dog, every 4 to 6 hours he needs to be let out – this is a perfect time to take a break from the computer screen, step outside get some fresh air, and just take a quick break to enjoy some time with the dog.

Distractions can be one of the most frustrating elements of working from home. Noisy neighbors cutting the grass, your dog barking at the neighbor cutting the grass, your kids asking you questions about the school work, and your spouse asking you a bunch of questions that seem pretty irrelevant in the given moment – all distractions. Make sure your family also understands that when you're at work, you're at work and not to interrupt you unless it is necessary.

You may have some distractions that you can push through and deal with in some kind of way.

However, there are situations such as the neighbor cutting the grass that you simply can't do anything about. You may have your own set of distractions that are unique to your location such as traffic noise, sirens and police activity or even noise from airplanes and helicopters.

These things can be tough to overcome which is why you may need to adjust your schedule to work when the majority of these noises and distractions are not taking place. There is simply no way to film or record professional video with the loud background noise taking place. This is one of the reasons why I recommend using acoustic treatment such as foam panels on the walls of your office or filming space.

Another important concept to understand in this chapter is that distractions are not just in the physical world they're also in the digital world. There are so many distractions that we face when on our computers. And you will constantly have competing priorities vying for your time and attempting to compel you off your current course of action.

It's important to stay focused on one specific task before moving on to another one - That's very similar to the concepts that you should take regarding our online businesses. Another words get one up and running or completed prior to starting something new.

Remember, Stay focused and you can do it.

Chapter 14: It Works

Making Your First Dollar

Making your first Dollar online is amazing feeling, it validates all your hard work, efforts, and belief in what you've been doing and what you've invested your time in.

Your products may not be the greatest when you start – this has been my experience thus far. However, your products will get better as you continue learning your online business. Just keep moving forward.

Is very important to develop what is known as proof of concept when you first start out – meaning the idea you had is worth someone buying. From a psychological standpoint it's also very important to have some small victories when you first start out to keep you motivated and driven to further success.

The more success you have, meaning the more sales that you have or the more money that you make, the greater your confidence level will be in the overall system and process that you're doing. This will give you even greater courage to reach out and expand your horizons to new possibilities to making money online.

My First Sale - My Experience

I'll never forget how excited I was making my first sale online. I had little comprehension about exactly what I was doing, but I knew enough to be able to publish my first book and make my first sale. Looking back it's amazing how much I've grown as an author and a publisher. My hope is to save you some much needed time, energy, and money along your journey to making money online with the use of this book.

When I made my first sale online I almost couldn't believe that I did it. The more that I published, the more that I made sales but it was that initial sale that made me actually realize that making money online is possible – and I can do it. And just as I can do it, you can do it as well – it works!

Chapter 15: Income

There are two types of income I will discuss in this chapter – Passive Income and Active Income.

Some of you may be wondering what in the world is passive income and what is active income - I thought income was income. So did I not too long ago – but when I found out about this mysterious thing called passive income it changed my life. I look at passive income as income that you earn with little to no effort on your part to maintain. Please note I used the word, "Maintain" for reason.

Any type of digital product is a great example of one way to generate passive income. Take for instance this very book – now it's taken me some time and effort initially to write the material, edited it, and publish it in its various forms.

However, once it's completed and placed on the various platforms such as Amazon, Barnes & Noble's, Google play, IBooks, and Audible there is nothing more I need to do to the actual product. Additionally with Digital Products there is no inventory to maintain which is pretty awesome if you think about it.

Passive income is something that initially takes a lot of hard work and planning to get going. However, once the products have been created and placed on various marketplaces, the sales will organically come in if you have a decent product.

It should be noted here that passive income cannot be accomplished by selling a service. Any service that you provide will require you to trade your time for money and as a result you can never hope to generate passive income from it. A service that you provide would be an example of active income. Active income is just that, it's you being active in trading your time and skill for money.

There is nothing wrong with active income. I think for most of us this is generally how we make most of our money. In this next chapter I will discuss various online businesses that are both passive and active.

Chapter 16: Online Businesses

There are numerous types of online businesses that you can start and many have a very low barrier to entry. I will highlight four primary ways that I make money online as I believe these are the easiest to get started with. In my opinion these four options also give you the best possible return on your initial investment of time and money.

Self-Publishing

Self-publishing is what I started out with and is the number one online business I would recommend was starting out. You can self-publish through companies like Amazon, Smashwords, Draft2Digital, Google play, and more.

Self-publishing gives you the best return on your initial investment of time or money. With one book you can develop multiple streams of income to help ensure your return on investment. You can publish your one book in the following ways:

- E-book
- Paperback
- Hardback
- Audiobook

And even within your E-book you can develop multiple streams of potential revenue by publishing on various platforms that accept E-books. Specifically for your E-books you can publish one book on the following platforms:

- Amazons KDP
- Google play

- Smashwords or Draft2Digital which will distribute your books to major retailers such as Barnes & Noble's, iBooks, and Scribed. Depending upon which aggregate publisher you use they will distribute your books to 8 to 14 different retailers.

In fact you could even take the contents of your book and develop an online course.

Online Course Creation

Online learning and online courses used to be something reserved for colleges and universities but no longer. Online learning is fast becoming the preferred way to gain practical knowledge on specific skills that students want to learn that directly relate to the life in some way.

Everyone comes to the table with their own set of unique skills, life experience, and passions. Therefore everyone has something that they can teach and share. As I mentioned previously if you are self-publishing then you could take the content from your book and turn it into an online course.

There are several places that you can publish your online courses. These places are online course marketplaces that are similar to Amazon. The two major online course marketplaces are Udemy and Skillshare.

There are pros and cons to online course marketplaces but if you wish to host your courses yourself there are two major companies that facilitate this. The two self-hosting companies are Teachable and Thinkific. I personally use Thinkific but have heard good things about Teachable as well.

Both companies have three different plans ranging from free to their premium plans.

If you're shy about putting your face on camera that's perfectly understandable. However, you can actually create a course and not be in the video. Some courses that you develop may consist of PowerPoint slides that have been saved in a video format. Another way to create a course without being in the video is through what is called screen sharing. Screen sharing is just with the name implies it's where you record your screen and voice as you complete your online teaching.

For any online course creation I highly recommend Camtasia and Snagit both by Tech Smith. I've used these programs for some time now and have been very impressed with the interface and the ease-of-use. There is a very low barrier to learning this particular software that I know it will tremendously help you so check it out when you can.

Oh one more thing – because you would be teaching online courses you will qualify for the educational discount so please don't forget that if you plan to buy it.

Freelancing

The previous two online businesses were both what is known as passive income. Freelancing, however, is what is known as active income. Most of us are very familiar with active income as most of us trade our time for money.

Yet even with active income we can still have a measure of flexibility. We can actually work whenever we want through freelancing websites. Freelancing websites are an amazing thing and allow you to freelancer skills out to the entire world.

It doesn't matter what your skills are whether it's writing, video creation, or voiceover narration professional freelancers are in high demand.

There are two major websites that I would recommend at the time of this writing to look for work as a freelancer. The two websites are Upwork and Fiverr. I have personally utilize these websites to hire ghostwriters and marketing experts. I've also used Fiverr to sell ad space on my Christian websites.

In fact I will be moving forward with creating additional gigs under my own name to get work as a freelance voiceover artist in the near future as I've just completed creating a vocal booth and investing in $1,000.^{00} microphone. Remember if you want something bad enough you go out and get it. The start of my voiceover career is yet another part of my overall strategic plan of action in my whole systems approach to my online business.

Blogging with Affiliate Links

Do you remember me mentioning how important having a centralized professional website is? Well the same holds true for any blog, especially if you attempt to monetize your blog or website. There are several ways that you can monetize your website or blog. A lot of people use Google ads help generate income.

However, placing Google ads on your website is not the greatest idea if you wish to generate real income. Putting Google ads on your website or blog may give the viewer the impression of a scammy unprofessional website that may have some kind of virus.

Remember first impressions of your website are huge! You have one chance to make a first impression and from that first impression develop trust within the viewer that will lead to potential sales in the future.

So make sure that your website or blog is professionally laid out, is very clean looking, and that it's not too busy.

Affiliate links are links to other people's products that you receive a percentage of the sale from if they click the link on your website or blog and buy the product. These affiliate links are placed in specific locations throughout your website.

When attempting to make money through your website or blog with affiliate links never promote something that you have not personally used or that goes contrary to your overall website or blog. Another words if your website or blog is about camping you don't want to have affiliate links related to interior design on your website or blog – keep the topic generally the same.

Normally you can expect to make between 5% and 15% in commission from any sales from affiliate links. Additionally you want to have what is known as deep linking between your website and the company that hosts the affiliate link. Make sure that there is a 60 to 90 day window, preferably 90 days that the link will remain active if someone clicks on it so you receive your commission.

There are several companies that host numerous other companies and act as a go-between to manage potential affiliates. Amazon Associates and Commission Junction are two of the more well-known companies that offer affiliate services.

If you're looking for a specific product from a manufacturer go directly to their website and search around specifically at the bottom of their website to see if they have an affiliate program available. If they do, walk through the process to get approved and start placing affiliate links on your website to earn money.

That's a pretty awesome deal considering you're not creating any products, you have no inventory, and you're providing no actual service other than a platform for perspective buyers to purchase items. That my friends is what you call true passive income.

Chapter 17: Picking a Business

We have discussed several online business options that are available to you – but how do you decide which business to start? The choices can be overwhelming at this phase of the process and can often time cause many people to stall out and the stop dead in their tracks with their ambitions.

Yet picking an online business to start doesn't have to be that complicated or that overwhelming. You have to understand yourself and your personality before you can even hope to pick an online business to start. Let's look at online courses for example. Would it make sense to start this business if you are camera shy or don't really want your face broadcasted to the world? Chances are if you have this type of reservation you're more introverted and most likely would do better with self-publishing online rather than creating online courses.

At the same time I would say that most of us are camera shy and there is a bit of an awkwardness when we first start filming ourselves. So try to know yourself as best as possible and push yourself past your comfort zones. Remember starting a new business online takes time to develop and you most likely will need to learn new skills.

So coming back around to the question, "how do you pick which online business to start" we need to examine a few more things. We need to think about what is realistic for us to accomplish. We also should ask yourself another very important question – Why not start more than one online business at the same time?

With technology being what it is today you have so many options in front of you with so little barriers to entry. The question is do you have the drive, determination, and endurance to be about your business in a real way – in a way that will give you success both now and in the future.

My advice to you is this, to pick three online businesses to start that you think you could realistically see yourself doing then take massive action to accomplish your goals. And in all your planning it's important not to get bogged down with over analyzing everything. Planning is definitely a critical part of your business and without proper plans, you are planning for problems – but don't let it stop you from taking action.

You have about five seconds to seize success when a thought comes to your mind - you have to take action immediately on it or your brain will disregard it as unimportant. This strategy is called Speed of Implementation and should be highly ingrained within your business practice.

Chapter 18: Stop Procrastinating and Take Action

Procrastinating, probably the number one reason that most people don't succeed in whatever they do. As we just mentioned in the previous chapter, Speed of Implementation is necessary for any success with your online business. Do not underestimate the importance of this practice.

But let's keep it real here, if you want to do something you'll do it, and if you don't want to do something you won't do it. You can make all the excuses that you want but when the rubber hits the road as they say, the bottom line is you didn't want to do something or you did want to do something because your actions will always follow your beliefs.

If I could give you one piece of advice, it would be to stop lying to yourself and to be honest with yourself about what you want to do and what you don't want to do and then move forward accordingly.

There's a great line in Star Wars where Yoda the old Jedi Master is teaching Luke Skywalker and he says, "Do or don't do – there is no try" that about sums it up to stop procrastinating and lying to yourself do it or don't do it because there is no try. If you want it bad enough seize the day, seize whatever time you can to accomplish your goals.

No excuses, No lies – Take Action Now! Remember Speed of Implementation.

Special Gift

God has a Gift for You! The Plan of Salvation:

There is no formal prayer of salvation as many churches would have you believe, God's Word is very clear - there is only one way to get to the Father in heaven and that is through Jesus Christ (John 14:6). Jesus says that you must be born again to enter into heaven (John 3:3-5).

Salvation is simply the first step in building an open and honest relationship with God. We all have sinned and fallen short, but there is Hope in Jesus Christ - Just cry out to God in sincerity and honesty asking for forgiveness and for Him to Save you, Sanctify you, and fill you with His Holy Spirit - Ask for His will to be done in your life on earth as it is in Heaven and That's it, now just keep it real with God.

A Warning:

The Christian walk is not an easy life on the surface. The Word of God says that we will be hated in all the world for Christ namesake (Matt. 24:9). The Bible says that in the last days are enemy prevail against us physically until Christ returns to save us (Dan 7:21, 22). Furthermore, we must endure hardship as a good soldier of Jesus Christ (2 Tim 2:3) and yet we are never alone in this, God promises us that He will never leave us nor forsake us if we believe in him (Matt.28:20).

In everything we go through we have the peace and joy of God which surpasses all understanding (Philp. 4:6-8) The Bible declares, "For I consider the sufferings of this present time are not worthy to be compared with the glory which shall be revealed in us". (Rom 8:18). However, in all these things we are more than conquerors through Jesus Christ (Rom. 8:37)

Stay In Contact

Stay in Contact with the American Christian Defense Alliance, Inc. through Our Website At: ACDAInc.Org

Join Our Mailing List

We also Greatly Appreciate You Signing Up For Our Mailing List and Providing a Good Rating and review for this Book. Your reviews help other people like yourself find this book on Amazon and benefit from its contents.

If You or Your Family have been Blessed by this book please let us know by dropping us a line through our website at acdainc.org

Find All Our Books

Wisdom from Your Elders:
Learning From Your Parents,
Grandparents, and the Older
People in Your Church

Prayer: Your No. 1 Prayer Book To
Learn To Be A Strong Christian
Prayer Warrior That Prays With
Powerful Prayers In The War
Room To Overcome And
Defeat The Enemy

Race Relations in America: A
Christian Guide

Martial Arts Ministry: How To
Start A Martial Arts Ministry

Biblical Bug Out: Don't Bug In -
Follow The Calling

Christian Prepping 101: How To
Start Prepping

How to Finance Your Full-Time RV
Dream

Additional Platforms

Thank you for reading this book. Your support and the support of others continue to enable our Ministry to grow. We hope and pray that this book has blessed you. If you enjoyed this book consider purchasing it on additional platforms or giving it as a gift to someone who could benefit from it.

We have this book available as an E-Book, Paperback, and Audio Book. We have no way to know which platform you purchased our book on but want to make you aware of another way you can help support our Ministry if you haven't yet listen to the audio book version of this book.

If you Enjoy Listening to Audio Books in General Consider Signing Up For Audible.com. If You've Been On the Fence About Signing Up for Audible.com or Would Just like to Support Our Ministry By Purchasing Our Audio Book First – We Would Greatly Appreciate It.

Did You Know that You Can Support Our Ministry By Listening to Our Audio Books on Audible.com?

Here's How:

- Sign Up as a New Aubdible.com Member

- Purchase Our Audio Book First and

- Stay an Audible.com Member for at least 61 Days

If You Follow these Simple Steps Our Ministry will Earn $25.00 - $50.00 Every Time This Process in Completed. The Amount we earn is based on if we have narrated the book ourselves or outsourced it to another narrator.

We Greatly Appreciate Your Support as Well as You Sharing this information, including links to our books on Audible.com with Others on Your Social Media Platforms

Thank You Once Again for Your Support; We Know God Will Bless You as You Have Blessed This Ministry